The CONSERVATION Project Book

Hilary Thomas & Shirley Thompson

Kent Trust for Nature Conservation

Artwork by Tessa Lovatt-Smith

Headway · Hodder & Stoughton

What on earth is conservation?

The natural world is under pressure. Every day between 50 and 100 **species** (kinds) of plants and animals may become **extinct**. Tropical rainforests are being bulldozed and burned, and the air is becoming more **polluted**. We are all part of the same world and we all need to look after it. Will *you* help? It's not too late!

  Conservation of the natural world means caring for our wildlife and wild places and protecting them from unnecessary damage and destruction. It also means using the Earth's natural **resources** wisely and without wasting them. We need to **conserve** the air we breathe, the water we drink and the soil in which we grow our food. We must help to keep the **balance of nature** rather than upset it.

  In this book, you will find lots of activities and projects to make you think about the world in which we live and the effect we have on the **environment** (our living and non-living surroundings). **Global** problems, like acid rain and the loss of the rainforests, can only be mentioned briefly but after reading about them here you may want to find out more.

NOW is the time to set a course to help save **Planet Earth!**

The environment and you

Much of what we do, use and throw away has some effect on our environment. How many times do you leave the TV on when nobody is watching it? Every time this happens **energy**, in the form of electricity, is wasted. This means wasting precious supplies of coal, oil or gas which are used to make the electricity.

Using paper is using trees. Do you waste trees? Every car journey adds more pollution to the air. Litter that you leave around is not only ugly but often dangerous, both to people and wild animals.

Our actions can also affect the environment in other parts of the world. For example, some of the beefburgers we eat are linked to the destruction of the tropical rainforests (find out how on page 25).

EVERY YEAR EACH BRITISH HOUSEHOLD THROWS AWAY AROUND ONE TONNE OF RUBBISH AND USES SIX TREES WORTH OF PAPER!

4 Ask your local library for the *Green Consumer Guide* or similar books giving the latest information on saving energy and resources.

Things to do

Recycle all you can.

1 Find out where your nearest bottle bank is. Don't just take *your* empties there, encourage your friends to do so too.
2 Does anyone near you collect old newspapers for recycling? If not, start a collection yourself. Ask your local Council where to take them.
3 Aluminium drinks cans can be recycled. Why not start a collecting point at school? Look up metal dealers in the *Yellow Pages* to find a buyer, or contact the Aluminium Can Recycling Association, 52 Blucher Street, Birmingham B1 1QU.

HOW TO MAKE RECYCLED PAPER

1. FRAME
Use two wooden frames of equal size (about 20cm x 15cm). Cover one with fine mesh netting.
top frame

2. PULP
Tear up paper and soak in warm water over night. Pulp with your hands or a potato masher to make a runny 'porridge'.

3. DIP
Dip your frame into the pulp and scoop up enough to leave an even surface on the netting.
top frame

4. PRESS + DRY
Remove top frame and gently turn paper on to a flat J-cloth.
J-cloth
Cover with another J-cloth and newspapers, and press down hard.
Uncover the sheets + leave to dry in a warm room.

Dictionary Check

Look up **recycle, resources, global**

Wildlife and wild places

We are all inhabitants of Planet Earth, together with millions of other plant and animal species. In the first part of this book, we take a look at some of the places where these plants and animals are found.

The place where an animal or plant lives is its **habitat** – a pond, the sea, a wood, a tree, or even under a stone. Habitats can easily be lost or destroyed. To conserve our wildlife species we need to look after, protect and **manage** the places where they live.

A pond is a good example of a habitat needing regular management. Left alone, it can become choked with vegetation or may even dry up. To keep a pond rich in wildlife, some vegetation needs to be cleared from time to time. This management work will ensure that there are always areas of open water.

A chain reaction

A wildlife habitat contains different species of plant and animal living together as a **community**. Each living thing needs energy to survive. Green plants use the sun's energy to make food. The animals then get their energy by eating plants (if they are **herbivores**) or from eating other animals (if they are **carnivores**).

The flow of energy from the sun through the plants and animals links them together in a **food chain**. However, some animals do not always eat the same thing and can therefore be in more than one food chain. As a result, food chains are linked together into **food webs**.

A WOODLAND FOOD WEB

Things to do

1   We are at the top of many food chains. Make a list of all the different foods you eat in one day. Work out the food chains you belong to.

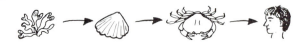

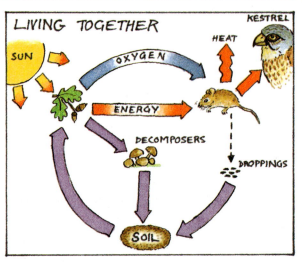

LIVING TOGETHER

2   Animals have their own territory or 'home range'. Draw a map of the area around your home from memory. Compare *your* home range with that of a friend. Do your territories overlap?

Dictionary Check
Look up **community**

Wild in the town

Yes, the town! If you live in a town, there is no better place to start finding out about wildlife than right on your own doorstep.

Towns provide plenty of food and shelter for those plants and wild creatures able to live in a man-made environment. As a result, many of our plants and animals are found in **urban** (built-up) areas.

IF ALL THE GARDENS IN BRITAIN BECAME ONE GIANT 'NATURE RESERVE', IT WOULD COVER MORE LAND THAN HALF A MILLION FOOTBALL PITCHES!

To a house martin, the wall of a building is no different from a natural cliff-face; both make excellent nest-sites. Discarded 'take-aways' make ready meals for the urban fox, and even kestrels take up residence on ledges of high-rise buildings.

Gardens can also provide habitats for birds, insects and other creatures able to **adapt** (fit in) to this kind of environment. Research by members of WATCH, the national environmental club for young people, has shown that garden ponds have become major spawning sites for the not so **common frog**. Without these ponds, the number of frogs would drop even more. If you have a garden and it doesn't have a pond, page 16 shows how you can make one!

Your **Conservation Action Plan**, in the centre of this book, shows you lots more ideas for making homes for wildlife.

How clean is your air? A lichen survey may tell you!

Lichens are plants often found growing on walls, gravestones and trees. They are very sensitive to air pollution, especially that caused by **sulphur dioxide**. Their presence or absence will give you a clue to how clean your air is! 'Crusty' lichens will tolerate *some* pollution, 'leafy' lichens are less tolerant and the 'shrubby' ones like only *clean* air. If you cannot find any lichens, you may have a real pollution problem!

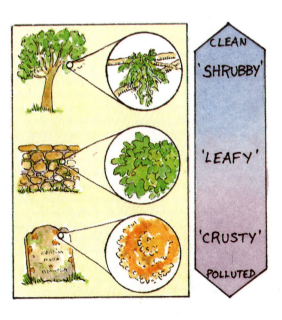

5

Street wild

In some areas of a town, you may find fragments or 'relics' of countryside left over when the town was built. Can you find an old hedge, a small piece of woodland, or a patch of meadow on land that has not been used for building? Use this evidence, together with old maps and photographs, to draw a picture or plan of how the area may once have looked. Names of old streets may give further clues, such as Woodside Road or Oakwood Lane. Do these areas of left-over countryside need protection from future development?

Old churchyards are good places for wildlife, often remaining quiet and undisturbed for centuries. Look for mosses and lichens on walls and gravestones, and wild flowers that survive where **herbicides** (weedkillers) have not been used. Ask permission to carry out a simple wildlife survey. Show your results to those who look after the area and ask them to help protect the wildlife living in their churchyard.

Railway and canal banks support many different kinds of plants and animals. Mice and voles find food and shelter here, needing to keep out of sight of any kestrel hovering above. Clearance of vegetation from a railway or canal bank may seem unnecessary. Try and persuade those responsible to leave at least one side undisturbed, then the habitat will not be destroyed completely. Get the support of friends and neighbours who share your views. *Do not trespass on to railway or canal banks.*

How many food chains can you discover in the picture above? Use the chains to make your own **urban food web**.

Derelict or 'waste' ground in a town can become an 'unofficial nature reserve'. Plants like ragwort, rosebay willowherb and buddleia not only bring colour but also attract insects. Soon a whole wildlife community settles in. Adopt a piece of waste ground and, with the help of others, make it your own **natural park**. Remember to get the owner's permission first! This book gives you lots of ideas for creating and managing habitats (see centre pull-out).

Roadside verges in towns are often mown regularly to keep the grass short. If left to grow longer, grass will give shelter to small mammals and wild flowers will have time to bloom. The flowers in turn will encourage insects. Write to the local Council and ask them to leave at least some verges uncut through the summer.

Buildings provide different mini-habitats. Walls and roofs are ideal for mosses and lichens (which do they prefer, sun or shade?). Cracks and crevices provide a home for minibeasts. Starlings frequently roost in their thousands on buildings, whilst under the eaves and behind tiles bats may also be found. In recent years there has been a drop in bat populations and they are now protected by law. If you know of a place where bats roost, tell your local Bat Group. They can be contacted via your County Wildlife Trust.

7

Wildlife watching in your garden

As wild creatures are encouraged to your garden, observe and discover more about their daily lives.

Provide food and water for birds throughout the winter. A variety of food in different places will attract more species. Discover which food different birds prefer. Watch to see who chases off whom. Are some of the bullies themselves bullied by others?

milk cartons make simple and cheap bird feeders.
Make several and paint them a variety of colours.
Use the cartons to see which foods are most popular.
— Do the birds have a colour preference?

A flower border full of nectar-rich plants like marjoram, thyme, foxglove and chicory will attract bees, butterflies and many other insects. Which are the most popular colours? Night-scented flowers such as honeysuckle are attractive to moths. These in turn are food for bats.

Discover which plants attract the most insects. Does the weather or time of day affect the number of insects seen? Investigate how long different insects spend on different plants. Is there a pattern to their behaviour?

Hedgehogs probably already visit your garden in search of slugs and other juicy morsels. *Never* poison their food by putting down slug pellets. Add to their natural diet, especially in autumn, by putting out bread, dog food and diluted milk or water. They will take this in addition to their natural diet (for more information read *Hedgehogs* by Pat Morris).

Mark your visiting hedgehog with a **tiny** spot of **non-toxic** paint. You may find 'your hedgehog' is actually several! How often does the same one return?

Pile up logs or brushwood, and build a compost heap. These are valuable habitats. Never sweep up all the dead leaves in autumn. They are needed as winter nesting material for hedgehogs and small mammals, as well as food and shelter for minibeasts.

HEDGEHOG SHELTERS

A log pile with plenty of dry leaves

A paving slab or plank of wood covering a dip in the ground, with lots of dry leaves.

Dictionary Check
Look up **toxic**

Wild woods

Exploring a wood is like exploring a town! Everywhere, you will see homes of different shapes and sizes and hear the hustle and bustle of daily life.

BETWEEN ⅓ AND ½ OF THE ANCIENT WOODLAND FOUND IN BRITAIN 50 YEARS AGO HAS BEEN DESTROYED.

The most exciting woods are those containing a mixture of our **native** trees (those species that have been found in Britain for thousands of years).

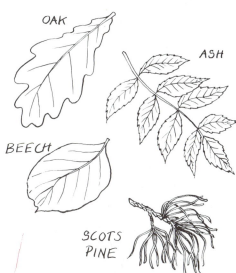

OAK

ASH

BEECH

SCOTS PINE

Many more wildlife species depend on these native trees than on trees that have been 'introduced' from abroad. **Ancient woods**, those that are hundreds of years old, are the most valuable of all to wildlife. Here, the wildlife community may include up to 4000 or 5000 different types of plants and animals.

Beneath the trees grow flowers such as bluebells and wood anemones, and woodland grasses. Ferns and mosses thrive in damper areas of the woodland floor, while fungi can be seen on living and dead wood. These, with the trees and shrubs, provide food and shelter for birds, insects and other animals.

Sadly, over the years many of our woods have been cleared to make room for houses, roads, factories and farmland. This is still happening. Imagine how many creatures lose their homes *every* time a wood or even just one tree is cut down.

Protecting and caring for our woodlands is one of the most important jobs for wildlife **conservationists.**

Study an oak tree and you will find it teeming with life. Here are just a few of the things you might see. Fit the names on to the grid – and reveal one more!

Life in a wood

Much of the lowland areas of Britain were once covered by broadleaf woodland. Most broadleaf trees, like oak, ash and beech, are deciduous, losing their leaves in winter. The leaves are 'broad' and flat unlike the 'needle-like' leaves of most coniferous trees (trees with 'cones'). Most coniferous trees are evergreen. Scots pine is one native conifer found in Britain. Our native broadleaf woods are home to many more plants and animals than the plantations of non-native conifers planted today. (Can you think of some reasons why?)

Many plants and animals live at the **edge of a wood**. With the extra sunlight here, more flowers are able to grow and these provide food for insects. Woodland birds like the blackbird prefer this part of the wood – feeding in the open but returning to the wood for shelter and safety.

Most of our **land mammals** were originally found in woods. Some, like foxes, have moved and adapted to other habitats as well. Others, like the dormouse, are still only found in woodland and as their habitat disappears, so do they!

Woodland flowers need sunlight to grow and many will bloom in the spring before the leaves of the trees shade the ground. Try to visit a wood when the leaves are just unfolding. Which trees come into leaf first? Leaves hang differently on different trees. Look upwards through the branches to see how this affects the amount of sunlight reaching the ground.

Many of our broadleaf woodlands have been **coppiced** in the past and some are still managed in this way. The trees are cut to ground level and then allowed to grow up again before being harvested 10 to 20 years later. The trees re-grow with several stems rather than one main trunk. Coppicing allows more light to enter the wood and this encourages woodland flowers. In turn these attract insects and other wildlife. Coppiced wood has a variety of uses including fencing posts, tool handles and firewood.

Things to do

1 Place names can sometimes give us clues as to where woods once stood that have long since disappeared. Use a map of your local area to hunt for clues. For example **leigh** and **ley** are Saxon words for a clearing in a wood.
2 Draw your own picture of wildlife in a wood, using coloured pens to link up the animals into food webs.
3 Use your local library to see if you can find out what animals might have lived in the wood 100 years ago, 1000 years ago and even 10,000 years ago!

Dictionary Check

Look up *nutrients, evergreen, plantation, invertebrate, decompose*

On the **woodland floor**, fallen leaves rot and decay returning 'food' or **nutrients** to the soil. These nutrients can be used again by the trees and other plants to help them grow. We call this the **cycle of decay**. Search the leaf litter for **invertebrates** and fungi as they help to **decompose** the leaves.

Make friends with a tree!

Carry out a study of a tree that you can visit regularly. Here are just a few things to discover about your tree:

Look at and sketch the shape of your tree.

Study leaf shapes and the pattern of the bark and think of some words to describe these.

Describe the feel and smell of the bark and the leaves.

Investigate the leaves and bark for insects and other minibeasts.

Shake one of the lower branches gently (if you can reach!) onto a white sheet. Examine any minibeasts that fall out. How many different ones can you see? Can you recognise any? Look at them closely and sketch those you find most interesting.

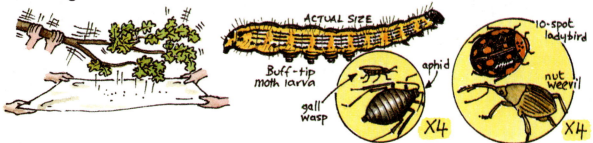

Search for signs of larger animals using your tree – a squirrel's **drey** or a bird's nest, for example. In how many different ways is your tree being used by animals?

Watch birds that visit your tree. How are they using it? Are they collecting food, nesting, or just sheltering? Are they singing to mark their territory?

Keeping a record of observations over a few weeks or even a whole year will give you a real picture of the fascinating **world of a tree**.

HOW TO PLANT A TREE

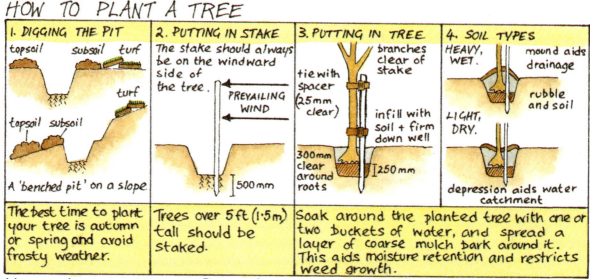

1. DIGGING THE PIT	2. PUTTING IN STAKE	3. PUTTING IN TREE	4. SOIL TYPES
topsoil subsoil turf / turf / topsoil subsoil / A 'benched pit' on a slope	The stake should always be on the windward side of the tree. / PREVAILING WIND / 500 mm	branches clear of stake / tie with spacer (25mm clear) / infill with soil + firm down well / 300mm clear around roots / 250 mm	HEAVY, WET. mound aids drainage / rubble and soil / LIGHT, DRY. / depression aids water catchment
The best time to plant your tree is autumn or spring and avoid frosty weather.	Trees over 5 ft (1·5 m) tall should be staked.	Soak around the planted tree with one or two buckets of water, and spread a layer of coarse mulch bark around it. This aids moisture retention and restricts weed growth.	

Always plant a native tree. Remember some can grow very tall. Make sure your tree is right for the site!

Wild and wet

To find out what the underwater world in our ponds and streams is really like, you would need to put on aqualung and fins and shrink to the size of your thumb! The aqualung would allow you to breathe air underwater, while your new size would help you fit into this world in miniature.

UP TO HALF OF THE PONDS FOUND IN BRITAIN 50 YEARS AGO NO LONGER EXIST.

What an exciting – and dangerous – world you would find! Even a small pond can be home to many different species of plants and animals. Rushes and reeds growing around the edge reach out above the water into the air. A forest of waving fronds houses creatures of extraordinary shapes and patterns. Thick stalks of water lilies lead up to the surface, their leaves forming platforms for animals lying in wait for their next meal. Below in the mud live creatures stranger than anything you could dream of, some grazing on plants, others hunting, swimming, crawling, or just sitting, watching for a chance to prey on an unfortunate companion.

Farm and village ponds were once needed as a water supply for a variety of uses including the watering of animals. With the introduction of water from a tap in most parts of Britain, many ponds have become neglected or filled in. Filling in just one pond can destroy the home of thousands of creatures.

Fortunately, new ponds are easy to establish and will quickly attract wildlife. By making even a small pond you will be doing something valuable for conservation (see page 16).

Life in fresh water

The number and variety of animals living in an area of water varies. It depends on whether it is a pond or stream, in sun or shade, large or small, what the soil is like and what part of the country it is in. We need to conserve our ponds and streams for many creatures depend on them. Some come only at breeding time, others visit regularly for food. Many insects and other invertebrates spend all or part of their lives in water. What would happen to each of the creatures pictured here if this pond was filled in?

All animals need to breathe in **oxygen** and this can be a problem to those living in water. Some, like the tiny water fleas, take in oxygen which has dissolved in the water through their skin. Gills enable some larger creatures to take in this dissolved oxygen too. Others go up to the surface to breathe or take bubbles of air, like tiny aqualungs, down with them. Which animals will die first if the water is so polluted that there is little oxygen in it?

Damselflies and dragonflies are among the many insects that spend only the earlier part of their lives in water. Find out more about their life-cycles.

All **amphibians** lay their eggs in water. Many **frogs** now depend on garden ponds for breeding as so many farm and village ponds have been lost. Many **toads** become road casualties as they migrate to their breeding ponds in early spring. Toad patrols and crossing signs have saved thousands. Will *you* help a toad across the road? Ask your County Trust how you can help.

Unseen **pollution** can be especially dangerous. **Chemicals** may drain through the soil from farm or industrial land, or be poured directly into rivers and streams, threatening freshwater life.

While decomposition of animal and plant remains is important in nature's cycle of decay, too much waste overloads the system. **Sewage** pumped into the water can upset the balance as the bacteria breaking it down use up too much oxygen. If you see signs of extreme pollution, such as a number of dead or dying fish, contact your local Council or the National Rivers Authority.

Ponds can be deep! Take care when studying a pond and never go alone.

Fishing tackle kills many birds and other animals. If you go fishing, never leave broken tackle or litter. When walking by a river take a carrier bag with you to collect other people's discarded tackle. (Mind your fingers!) Look on overhanging trees as well as on the ground.

Small mammals can easily become trapped in tins and bottles. Organise a campaign to clear litter.

Dictionary Check

Look up **amphibian, pollution, sewage**

Things to do

1   Be a Water Investigator. Look around your neighbourhood. What ponds are there? Do they look healthy? How might it be possible to improve them? Seek the owner's permission for a group of you to help clear a local pond or stream (you may need some adults to help you). Ask for advice on pond management from your County Wildlife Trust.

2   Write to WATCH (address on back cover) and see if they are running any pond projects or surveys that you can join in with.

Action for ponds

Among the plants in your pond include some that are fully submerged. These are very important as oxygenators and can include water milfoil, curled pondweed and water crowfoot. Plant in weighted bags of mud, dropped into the water. Flowering rush and water plantain planted near the water's edge provide shelter for pond animals. Marsh marigold and yellow flag are good 'marginal' plants providing valuable shelter for amphibians.

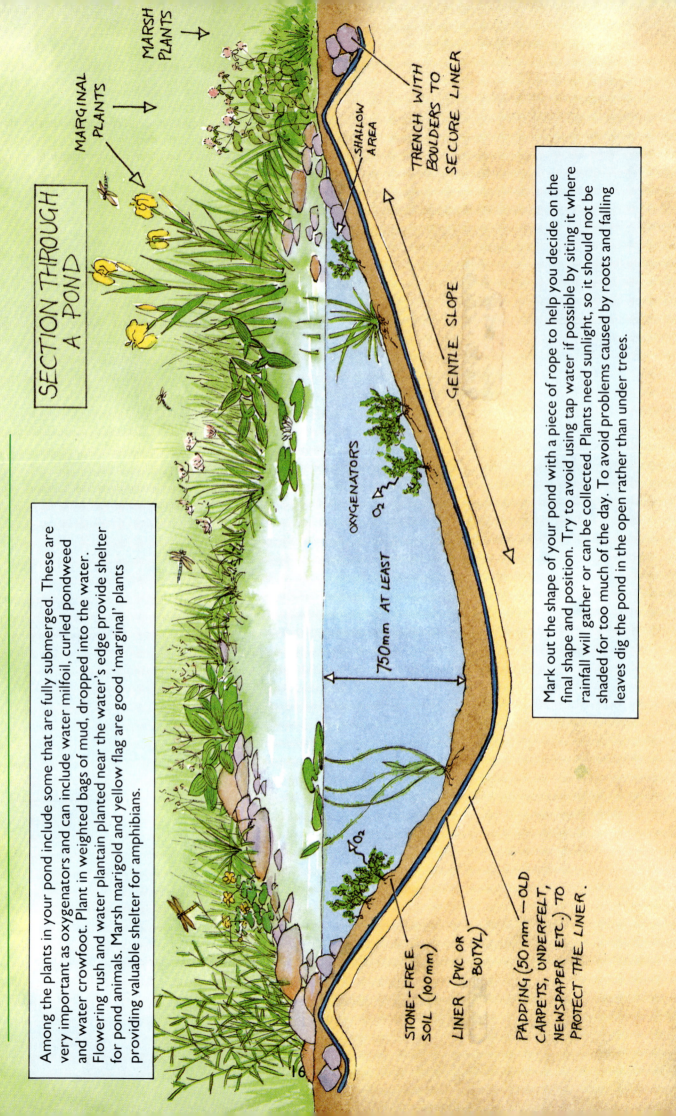

SECTION THROUGH A POND

MARSH PLANTS

MARGINAL PLANTS

SHALLOW AREA

TRENCH WITH BOULDERS TO SECURE LINER

OXYGENATORS

O_2

GENTLE SLOPE

750mm AT LEAST

STONE-FREE SOIL (100mm)

LINER (PVC OR BUTYL)

PADDING (50mm — OLD CARPETS, UNDERFELT, NEWSPAPER ETC.) TO PROTECT THE LINER.

Mark out the shape of your pond with a piece of rope to help you decide on the final shape and position. Try to avoid using tap water if possible by siting it where rainfall will gather or can be collected. Plants need sunlight, so it should not be shaded for too much of the day. To avoid problems caused by roots and falling leaves dig the pond in the open rather than under trees.

ACTION FOR WILDLIFE

BIRD BOXES

WOODLAND

WOODLAND EDGE

BRAMBLE

STINGING NETTLES

LEAF LITTER/ LOG PILES

LONG GRASS

POND OR BOG

WILDFLOWER MEADOW

FLOWER POT

Create a **wildflower meadow.** Sow native wildflower seed or use plants (available from good garden centres). Cut the meadow in summer after the flowers have seeded and rake off the cuttings.

An upturned and half-buried **flower pot** makes an ideal nest site for a bumble bee. Add some dry moss for bedding.

Bird boxes make additional nest sites with different designs attracting different species. Special boxes can also provide roost sites for bats.

Creating new habitats and looking after or managing existing habitats are two ways in which you can help wildlife conservation. Encourage wildlife to your window box, balcony, garden, school grounds or local piece of waste ground. This Action Plan shows you how to do it.

HEDGEROW

WINDOW BOX

SCENTED FLOWERS

IVY

A **window box** planted with nectar-rich flowers such as marjoram, chives and thyme will attract bees and butterflies (and double up as a herb garden!). Hang bird feeders from the window box in winter.

Leaf litter and **log piles** give shelter to minibeasts. A pile of dry dead leaves may attract a hibernating hedgehog.

For your **woodland,** plant native trees for maximum wildlife value, e.g. oak, birch, willow, ash, alder, beech. Check which suits your soil.

For your **woodland edge,** plant shrubs with nuts or berries to provide for birds and small mammals, e.g. hazel, spindle, guelder rose.

Create a **pond** or **bog** area (see page 16). Include plenty of plants around the edge to provide shelter for amphibians.

Keep some areas of **long grass** as shelter for minibeasts and small mammals.

Plants like honeysuckle that give off a **scent at night** will attract night-flying moths. These in turn are food for bats.

Ivy growing up a wall or fence provides food, shelter and nest sites for birds and a supply of nectar and pollen in late season for insects.

Bramble provides nectar for bees and butterflies. The blackberries are a food source for birds and small mammals. This prickly bush is also an ideal nesting habitat.

A small patch of **stinging nettles** will provide food for the caterpillars of the peacock, red admiral, comma and small tortoiseshell butterflies. Always cut some back to allow lots of young nettles to grow.

A **hedgerow** provides a home for nesting birds and small mammals. Plant with native species like hawthorn, blackthorn, beech and field maple.

Wild on the seashore

The **seashore** is a dangerous place to make one's home. Animals living there may be covered by salt water for part of every day and night, often with waves crashing over or tugging at them. When the **tide** is out, they may have to cope with hot summer sun, cold winter winds, or heavy rain.

BRITAIN DUMPS MILLIONS OF TONNES OF SEWAGE AND OTHER WASTE MATERIAL INTO THE SEA EVERY YEAR.

As if that didn't make life difficult enough, animals must search for food while trying to make sure they don't become someone else's dinner! All these problems have been tackled in various ways by plants and animals around our coast.

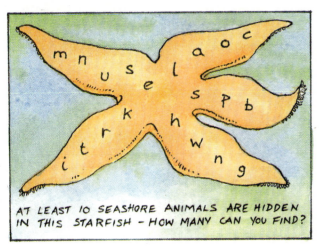

AT LEAST 10 SEASHORE ANIMALS ARE HIDDEN IN THIS STARFISH - HOW MANY CAN YOU FIND?

Wherever you explore, from rocky shore to sandy beach, you will find different wildlife communities. These communities vary a great deal and because of the constantly changing tide, most **marine** plants and animals can only survive in a narrow **zone** or section of the beach.

The very sea that can at times be rough and dangerous is still the source of food for animals living on the seashore. Millions of tiny **plankton** (single-celled plants and minute animals) drift in the water. These are at the base of the **seashore food chain**. Many animals filter this plankton from the water, only to be eaten in turn by others. Some seashore carnivores use up very little energy in movement, like the sea anemone which sits and waits for its dinner to swim past! As a result, food chains on the seashore often have more links than those on the land.

Our seas and shores are threatened by many forms of pollution, often unseen. Seashore animals and plants are particularly sensitive, so we need to be alert to any changes that might affect them.

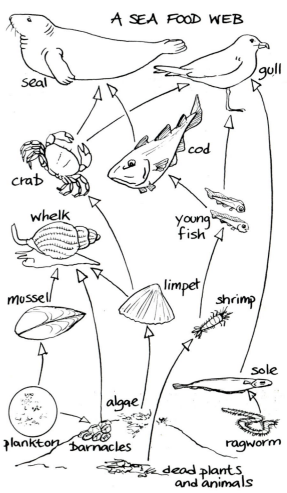

A SEA FOOD WEB

seal · gull · crab · cod · whelk · young fish · mussel · limpet · shrimp · sole · plankton · algae · barnacles · ragworm · dead plants and animals

17

Life on the shore

At the edge of the sea, where waves and wind mix air and water, there is plenty of dissolved oxygen in the water. As a result, many different animals live here.

Seaweeds absorb nutrients from seawater and use energy from sunlight as it filters through the water. They may be red, green or brown (see p.20).

Estuaries (where a river meets the sea) are particularly valuable places for birds. Thousands visit them in winter, feeding on the plants and minibeasts living there. Much of the land around our estuaries is now used for industry and farming and the water is polluted. Other areas are under threat. Use your school library to find out more about estuaries and their value for wildlife.

Worms live in the mud and sand of bays and estuaries. At low tide they hide in tunnels or tubes, but come out to feed as the tide comes in. Large-scale bait-digging for fishing can disturb feeding birds, keeping them away from their much-needed meal.

Most people enjoy searching for seashells on the beach. These belong to a group of animals known as **molluscs**. Their shell helps to protect them from winds, waves and **predators**. Some, like the dog whelk, are carnivores while others, like the cockle, filter food from the seawater. The limpets graze on seaweed growing on rocks, scraping it off with their strong tongues. Shellfish are seriously affected by pollution; some are killed directly, others are unable to breed successfully.

Things to do

1   Make a **survey** of man-made rubbish on the beach to help discover the culprits. Organise regular beach clearances if you live near the sea. By collecting rubbish you can save lives. (Always use gloves.) Ask the local paper to publicise what you are doing and why.

2   If you visit a harbour find out what **fish** are found in the area. Ask fishermen how catches compare with those of 10 or 20 years ago. Are some types of fish no longer caught? Pollution, over-fishing and the taking of young fish have all led to a reduction in fish stocks. Make more people aware of this by talking about your findings.

3   **Whales** and **dolphins** are now rarely seen around most of our coast. Surveys are finding out more about what is happening to them. Send a report of any sighting you make to the Cetacean Group, University of Oxford, Oxford, OX1 3PS. Ask grandparents and older friends when and where they remember seeing them in the past, and send that information in too.

Dictionary Check

Look up **predator, marine**

The **breakdown** of plant and animal remains is an important part of nature's cycle. However, when decomposing sewage is discharged into the sea the balance is upset. Less sensitive animals thrive while many others die.

We all enjoy being on or near the beach – but trampling and disturbance can be harmful to wildlife. **Always** replace rocks and the animals you have found under them. Keep away from places where birds are nesting. Write to the Marine Conservation Society for a copy of their Seashore Code (address on back cover).

Litter washed up on the beach includes rubbish dumped from boats, and damaged nets and tackle from fishing vessels. Plastic kills many thousands of animals; bags, netting, ring-packs and foam choke and entangle birds, turtles, seals and others.

Investigate the seashore

If you live near the sea or go on a seaside holiday in Britain, make a detailed study of the seashore.

Consult the tide table and travel out with a falling tide recording the different seaweed zones and the animals you find. Remember that the seashore can be a dangerous place and the tide may come in **very quickly**.

Search underneath and on seaweeds, under rocks and in pools. Watch animals in their homes but do not disturb them.

Note carefully what you see and where you find it. Don't worry too much about names – careful sketches and descriptions that anyone can understand are more useful.

By **comparing** records made at different times, you may be alerted to changes. Perhaps numbers of certain species may be dropping or the balance of different animals suddenly alters.

Contact the local County Wildlife Trust or the Marine Conservation Society if you are concerned.

HOW TO PRESS SEAWEEDS

1. FLOAT THE SEAWEED IN A TRAY OF SHALLOW WATER. SLIP PAPER UNDER SEAWEED

2. ARRANGE THE FRONDS WITH A PAINTBRUSH.

3. CAREFULLY DRAIN OFF WATER

4. LABEL YOUR SEAWEED. COVER WITH GAUZE AND PRESS BETWEEN NEWSHEETS UNDER A HEAVY WEIGHT.

5. AFTER A WEEK IT SHOULD BE READY FOR DISPLAY.

IRISH MOSS

PEPPER DULSE

SEA-LETTUCE

Seaweeds often have beautiful patterns, and while the brown ones are usually too bulky to preserve well, the reds and greens are fun to press and dry.

Try to find loose weed, *never* pulling the **holdfast** (they have no roots, they just hold fast) off the rocks.

With a hand lens and a good identification book or *field guide* you may like to try to identify the more common ones.

Changes in nature

Nature is changing all the time. Sometimes the changes are quick and we notice them; others are slow and may take many years. Some are natural, like the changes with the seasons. Others, like the cutting down of trees, result from the actions of people.

Then

Now

Things to do

1 How much has an area of countryside that you know changed? See if you can discover old photos and maps (try the local library). Make your own record of the past and present using photos, maps, sketches or even a collage. Do you like the changes you see in your 'past' and 'present' pictures? What sort of changes would you like to see in the future?

2 If you are unhappy about a planned change – for example, the building of an office block on a site you know to be important for wildlife – then write to your Council Planning Office. Your local paper may also be interested in your views.

Perhaps if we know more about what areas were like in the PAST, we can make the right changes NOW and help ensure our wildlife will be safe in the FUTURE!

What on Earth are we doing?

An oak tree that gives food and shelter to a squirrel may later be helped by the animal to spread its seeds. Acorns collected and buried for a winter store are often forgotten, and left to grow into young oak trees. Yet, at another time, the same squirrel may cause damage by stripping bark from the tree. So all living things affect, or are affected by their environment. Humans have more power to affect their surroundings than any other living thing.

Until a few thousand years ago people in Britain lived by gathering wild fruit and roots, and hunting fish, birds and other animals for food. They knew when and where to look for food, how to make a shelter, and how the animals around them lived. There were fewer people and any changes they made were gradual. In remote parts of the world, a few groups of people still live in this way, in balance with their environment.

However, in very recent times, in many parts of the world, people are making great changes very quickly. Today, in Britain, even those of us living in a tiny village in the country usually know little about our environment. Few of us would be able to eat without a visit to a shop to buy food, or know how to cook it without gas or electricity! Our homes were built by others and are full of things we take for granted, from water out of a tap to televisions. Yet to our great-grandparents these would have seemed like magic!

What effect is all this having on our environment? By ignoring our place in the **web of life**, we run the risk of upsetting nature's balance. In the second part of the book we will try to see how this may be happening now, and what we can do about it.

The study of the way plants and animals live together and affect each other is called **ecology**.

How many 'wildlife hazards' can you spot in this picture?

Making poetry, music and drama out of a crisis!

Have you read the poem on the inside front cover of this book? Write your own poem about something you care about or are concerned about – the loss of the rainforests perhaps or a piece of land near you threatened with the bulldozers.

Try lying under a tree looking up through the leaves to the sky. Write down all the words that come into your head. Use these words to create a poem about the tree. Get together with some friends and make a book of poems about the environment – you could even sell copies to raise money for a conservation project.

Create and act out your own TV advert about an 'environmentally friendly' supermarket, household or garden product.

Join with a team of friends and launch your own **school wildlife magazine**. Decide who will be responsible for different parts of the magazine, what the content will be, the title, who will write articles for it, how it will be printed, and so on. With more and more people taking an interest in wildlife your magazine could be a real winner!

The words below are from a song written by the TV presenter and conservationist Chris Baines, in aid of the British Wildlife Appeal. There have been many songs written about the effect we are having on our environment. Try writing your own song – and give a performance at school!

We have to decide what our wildlife is
*   worth*
As the hedges we've lost stretch three
*   times round the Earth*
We've lost half of our wetlands and
*   half of our trees*
And there's no meadows left for the
*   birds and the bees*
With motorways slicing their way
*   through the scene*
And pipelines so slick you can't see
*   where they've been*
Our countryside faces a pretty grim
*   fate –*
And we've got to act now 'cos
*   tomorrow's too late!*

How strange that a heron
who nests in trees
Can only eat dinner
when up to his knees
In water............

Down on the farm

Many years ago. . . . .

Early farmers learned to grow and improve plants for food, and to herd and fence animals. Over hundreds of years farming changed much of Britain's scenery. Woodland was cleared to make room for grazing animals or growing crops. New habitats were created including hedgerows, meadows and farm ponds.

Farming today

After the Second World War (when your grandparents were about your age!) there was a shortage of food. Farmers had to find ways of producing more and more to feed a growing **population.** This led to many changes in farming, changes that were made very quickly. Hedgerows were pulled up to make fields larger. This made it easier to use the big new farm machines. Chemicals were used to **fertilise** the soil. Weeds, insects and other 'pests' were killed with new chemical sprays. Marshland was drained to make extra space to grow still more food.

Food for thought!

The old-fashioned or **traditional** methods of farming allowed many different plants and animals to survive. While modern farming produces more food for people, many of the wildlife habitats created by farming in the past have been lost.

Chemicals used in pesticides can be passed on along food chains. This may lead to animals being poisoned – and that could also mean us!

The EC (European Commission) has set a safety level on the amount of **nitrates** (a form of nitrogen) allowed in drinking water. One source of nitrates is farm fertilisers. Find out more about how nitrates get into our drinking water.

Things to do

Find out about 'natural' ways of controlling garden 'pests' instead of using chemical pesticides. Write to the Henry Doubleday Research Association, National Centre for Organic Gardening, Ryton-on-Dunsmore, Coventry CV8 3LG, for information on organic gardening.

Dictionary Check

Look up **population, fertiliser**

WORLD ISSUE: TROPICAL RAINFORESTS

Tropical rainforests are luxuriant forests found in hot wet areas of the world. They are home to more than half of all the world's plant and animal species, animals like the jaguar, tapir and gorilla. Many **indigenous** (native) people have also lived in the forests for thousands of years.

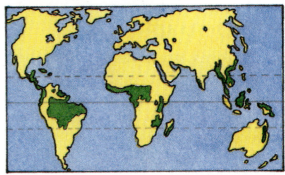

The world's tropical rainforests

The forests must live

Today, however, the forests are being destroyed at an alarming rate. *On average, an area the size of more than 10 football pitches is cleared every minute by bulldozing and burning.* Already, the world has lost nearly half of the rainforest that existed at the beginning of this century. At this rate, it could all be gone half way through your lifetime. How much has been destroyed since you started reading this book?

One reason for the destruction of the forests is to provide land for agriculture, including grazing land for beef cattle. Some of this meat is sold to make millions of beefburgers eaten every year in Britain and other countries.

Rainforest plants have given us many cures for diseases, including a treatment for childhood leukaemia. We are losing medicines and foods before they have even been discovered!

The rainforest people are threatened with the loss of their home and way of life.

As the trees burn, carbon dioxide is given off, adding to the problem of **global warming** (see *Living in a Greenhouse*, page 31).

Things to do

1 Use a modern atlas or large scale map of the world to find out the names of the three lines marked on the map above. In which countries are the tropical rainforests found? Use the information to draw your own rainforest map.
2 Visit the library to find out which animals are found in different areas of rainforest. Illustrate your map with pictures of some of these.
3 Make a list of things we use that come from tropical rainforests. Organisations like Friends of the Earth and WWF will help you. Does our use of these products harm the rainforest?

The cost of living

Many years ago. . . . .

As villages grew into towns, problems grew with them: food had to be transported from where it was produced. Fresh water was often not available. Fuel for cooking and heating had to be brought in, while sewage and other wastes had to be taken out of the town. Disease and ill health were common in overcrowded towns.

Living today

As a result of a global transport network, fresh, frozen and tinned food is easy to obtain in most parts of Britain. Coal, wood, gas, oil or electricity for heating are widely available and the majority of homes are supplied with electricity for lighting and other uses. Most of us have piped drinking water in the home, and flush toilets and regular rubbish collections are taken for granted.

Convenience – at a price!

It is easy to ignore the hidden costs of our convenient but sometimes extravagant way of life in this country.

Many important wildlife habitats have been used as building land.

We produce huge amounts of household rubbish, often unnecessarily. This wastes resources and can be difficult to get rid of.

Rivers and coastal waters are polluted by sewage. This lowers the level of oxygen, making the water unsuitable for many plants and animals.

We take tap water for granted and frequently use far more than we need to.

Our constant demand for electricity means that the power stations which make it are adding more and more polluting gases to the air.

We **import** and **export** products that may pollute or damage the environment of other countries and threaten some wildlife species. (Write to organisations like Greenpeace, Friends of the Earth or the Worldwide Fund for Nature and see if you can join in with any international campaigns to help save endangered species like the elephant and the whale.)

Dictionary Check

Look up **import, export, biodegradable**

WORLD ISSUE: THE OZONE LAYER

Ozone 'friendly'

The ozone layer in the Earth's atmosphere protects us from most of the sun's dangerous ultra-violet (UV) rays. Scientists have discovered that this layer is not only getting thin in places, there are also holes appearing in it!

Too much UV light can cause skin cancer, eye damage and weaken the body's immune system that helps protect us from disease. It can also damage plants. If more and more UV light gets through, it could eventually threaten all life on Earth.

Scientists think that one major cause of the damage to the ozone layer is the use of man-made chemicals called **chlorofluorocarbons** or **CFCs.** Once in the atmosphere, CFCs release chlorine which destroys the ozone. CFCs have been widely used in aerosols in the past. They can also be found in the cooling system of fridges and are used to 'puff-up' the plastic foam of polystyrene food containers. Even if CFCs are banned completely in the next few years, their effect will carry on well into the next century.

Make sure everything you use is 'ozone friendly'!

Things to do

1   Write to WATCH for details of their 'Ozone Project' (address on back cover).
2   Help conserve our energy supplies. If we insulate lofts, lag pipes, close doors, switch lights and heaters off when not needed, it all helps. Write to the Government's Department of Energy, Thames House South, Millbank, London SWIP 4QJ for information on energy conservation.

    Find out about safer and 'renewable' sources of energy, such as hydro-electric, solar, wind and tidal power. Write to the Centre for Alternative Technology, Machynlleth, Powys SY20 9AZ for their publications list.
3   Many beaches are considered unsafe places to sit or swim because of the risks from sewage. Complain to the local Council, or write to the Marine Conservation Society for advice, if you see evidence of pollution at home or on holiday.
4   Alert the National Rivers Authority or the Council's Environmental Health Department if you suspect pollution in a local river or stream.
5   'Environmentally friendly' household products such as **biodegradable** washing powders are now available which help to reduce the pollution of our rivers. Find out where they can be bought near your home – and encourage your family and friends to use them!

On the move

Many years ago. . . . .

Before the time of your great-grandparents few people, other than merchants or soldiers going to war, travelled away from their home town or village.

The railway train gave ordinary people the opportunity to explore farther afield, with a network of railway lines reaching every corner of the British Isles. However, it was the invention of the petrol engine and the aeroplane that led to the transport boom.

Travel today

Today people have cars, lorries, buses, motor-bikes, aeroplanes, and even spacecraft (and space junk – but that's another story!). We use cars (17 million of them in 1988) to travel to work, to school, to save time going just down the road, or to visit relations hundreds of miles away – and the number of cars is forecast to double in 20 years!

The road to ruin?

Motorways, car-parks, railways, canals, airports and docks all use up land that was once home to wildlife. Habitats are destroyed by quarrying for the stone and rock needed to make those roads.

Many places that used to be quiet and undisturbed are now regularly visited by tourists. This has lead to disturbance and damage in wild places.

The transport of oil, much of it for use in petrol and diesel engines, puts wildlife at risk. Oil spills at sea affect marine animals and coastal birds, while inland pipelines endanger more habitats.

As petrol is burnt in cars it produces **carbon monoxide, lead** and other exhaust fumes which pollute the atmosphere. Each year there are more and more cars on Britain's roads. In 1989, the Government declared yet another major road-building programme costing billions of pounds. Think how much countryside is lost for every extra mile of motorway built!

1993 should see the opening of the **Channel Tunnel**. To cope with the extra traffic, a new railway and new roads are planned for south-east England, threatening more wildlife habitats.

Acid raindrops kill!

Rainwater is normally slightly **acidic**. It can become more acidic when gases given off by burning **fossil fuels** dissolve in it. Even without rain these gases, particularly **sulphur dioxide** and **nitrous oxides**, can have a serious effect on our environment. The main sources of these gases are coal-burning power stations. However, car and lorry exhausts are increasingly adding to the problem.

Air pollution, including acid rain, is now being linked to tree damage and the loss of wildlife species in lakes and rivers across many parts of the world. In northern Britain and Scandinavia (find this area in your atlas), thousands of lakes are **acidified** and hold few wildlife species. In Wales, the **dipper** has declined in numbers because the freshwater insects that this bird eats have been lost. Breeding ponds of the rare **natterjack toad** in southern Britain are no longer suitable, and lichens and grassland species are disappearing from some areas (carry out your own lichen survey – see page 5).

Things to do

1 Test for yourself the level of acidity in the rain near your home. You can buy an acid rain testing kit from WATCH (address on back cover). Notice whether local buildings show signs of stonework being dissolved away.

2 Carry out a survey of traffic on a road where you can watch safely. How many cars pass in 30 minutes at different times of the day? How many of them have empty seats? How many buses and lorries? If the traffic is a problem in your street, can you think of ways of 'calming' the traffic down? Send your ideas to the local Council or newspaper.

3 To help reduce lead pollution in the air, ask your parents to use unleaded petrol in the family car. Encourage others to do the same. Think about how to use the family car less. Could you use the train more often? Walk more! Is your lift *really* necessary? (Around 3 out of every 4 car journeys in Britain are less than 5 miles long!)

4 Write to your local MP and ask what the Government and the EC are doing to help reduce pollution from car exhausts (find out about **catalytic converters**).

5 How many ways of non-polluting environmentally friendly travel can you think of (a skate board, a sailing boat . . .)? Can you invent a new method?

Dictionary Check

Look up **acidic**

The age of industry

Many years ago. . . . .

The Earth's natural resources, like stone, gold, lead, copper and iron, have been used in many ways for thousands of years. Energy from wind and water was sometimes used to make work easier.

It is only recently, in the more developed countries, that our whole way of life has come to depend so heavily on using the Earth's resources for industry and power.

Industry today

In Britain today, we expect to have cars and TVs, fridges, washing machines and even home computers. All these have to be manufactured. To do this, industry needs **raw materials** from which to make them and energy to drive machinery. The raw materials are often natural resources found in the ground and these have to be quarried or mined.

Most of the energy used in manufacturing comes from the burning of coal, oil and gas. These were formed from the remains of living things over millions of years and are known as **fossil fuels**.

The cost of our comfort

Many power stations and factories have been built on estuaries. Here, the land is flat and water is freely available. Transport is easy by river and sea. As a result, many important wildlife habitats in and around estuaries have been destroyed.

The environment has been damaged by mining for coal and minerals and quarrying for building stone, sand, clay and other raw materials. These raw materials cannot be renewed. As we use up those more easily reached, we need more energy to obtain further supplies.

Many industrial processes result in pollution of air, water and land. Some of the waste products are very toxic. Nuclear power stations also give cause for concern; for example, with the problem of having to store **radio-active** waste.

Is nuclear power environment-friendly, or not? Talk to people who are for and against it. Make your own decision.

Living in a greenhouse

High in the Earth's atmosphere, 'greenhouse' gases allow the sun's heat through to the Earth. These gases then act like a blanket, preventing some heat returning to space (like glass trapping heat in a greenhouse). Greenhouse gases include carbon dioxide (CO_2), nitrous oxide, chlorofluorocarbons and methane. As industry and power stations burn fossil fuels, more and more CO_2 is being released into the atmosphere, helping to increase this **greenhouse effect**. More CO_2 is released as the world's tropical rainforests are burnt. Scientists believe that methane gas given off from rice fields and livestock is adding to the problem.

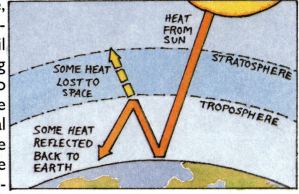

As this 'global warming' continues, the weather in many areas may become hotter and more unpredictable. The ice caps at the North and South Poles may melt, causing sea levels to rise much higher than they are now. Even a small rise in sea level could be disastrous for lowlying countries like Bangladesh, and small island countries in the Pacific Ocean could disappear!

In Britain, droughts and storms like the one that hit southern Britain in 1987 could become more common.

Launch into action!

SAVE ENERGY ... RECYCLE PAPER ... DRIVE LEAD-FREE ... RE-USE BOTTLES ...

MAKE your own contract, listing all the things that you intend to do to help Planet Earth! For example, taking bottles to the bottle bank. Try not to break your contract. Encourage your friends to draw up their own **Planet Earth contract!**

FIND OUT more about global environmental problems, like acid rain and the greenhouse effect. See what more *you* can do to help reduce these problems.

JOIN one of the many conservation and environmental organisations in Britain and help with conservation projects in *your* area.

PLANET EARTH NEEDS YOUR HELP NOW, IT'S NOT TOO LATE – BUT IT MIGHT BE SOON!

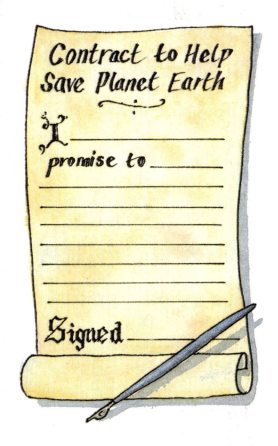

Go for green game board with the following spaces:

- DO YOU FEED THE BIRDS IN WINTER? ALWAYS +2 SOMETIMES -1 NEVER
- You take aluminium drinks cans for recycling +2
- WILD
- DO YOU TAKE UNNECESSARY PAPER BAGS IN A SHOP? NEVER SOMETIMES -1 ALWAYS
- You take bottles to bottle bank +2
- Your aerosol is not 'ozone friendly' -1
- WILD
- PINK and GREEN SPACES DO NOT COUNT IF YOU LAND THERE FROM A WILD SPOT.
- Do you pick up litter even if it isn't yours? ALWAYS +2 SOMETIMES -1 NEVER
- You plant a (native) tree +2
- Put slug pellets on the garden -1
- You dig a garden pond +2
- You join a conservation club +2
- WILD
- WILD
- You use the car for a short journey instead of walking -1
- Do you switch off a light when leaving a room? ALWAYS +2 SOMETIMES -1 NEVER
- You turn the heating up instead of putting on a jumper -1
- You make your own recycled paper +2
- START
- FINISH

Design your own **Green Game!** Use this example to help you. It can be as long and include as many 'spots' as you like.

How to play

The game is for two players. You will need a dice and a counter each. Take turns to throw the dice. If you land on a 'green' or 'red' spot, the number in the square tells you whether to go forward or back. If you land on a 'wild' spot you must answer the question honestly! Keep a count of how many times you each have to go back a square.

The winner is the player who has to go back the least number of times and therefore the one who has caused least environmental damage. You do not have to be first to the end to win!

A Green Survey!

Use the green spots to help you design your own survey and find out how 'green' your friends are! Here are some questions to help you get started. Try and think of about 10 altogether and work out a score for each answer

Qu. Do you take bottles to the bottle bank?
always 2 points   *sometimes* 1 point   *never* 0 points

Qu. Does your family car run on unleaded petrol?
yes 2 points   *no* 0 points

Tell each person their score. Encourage those with a low score to think more about the damage they may be doing to the environment.